W9-DFG-650

DATE DUE

MAY 24 2012			
DEC 29 2014			
JUL 27 2016			
GAYLORD		PRINTED IN U.S.A.	

I Like Sports Stars!

Read About
Eli
Manning

David P. Torsiello

Enslow Elementary

an imprint of

Enslow Publishers, Inc.

40 Industrial Road
Box 398
Berkeley Heights, NJ 07922
USA

http://www.enslow.com

For Mike Findlay: Remember that playoff game against the Panthers? On second thought, let's not.

Enslow Elementary, an imprint of Enslow Publishers, Inc.

Enslow Elementary® is a registered trademark of Enslow Publishers, Inc.

Library of Congress Cataloging-in-Publication Data

Torsiello, David P.
  Read about Eli Manning / David P. Torsiello.
    p. cm. — (I like sports stars!)
  Includes bibliographical references and index.
  Summary: "Eli Manning is the quarterback for the New York Giants. He loves to throw the football. He likes winning games even more"—Provided by publisher.
  ISBN 978-0-7660-3832-5
  1. Manning, Eli, 1981-–—Juvenile literature. 2. Football players--United States--Biography--Juvenile literature. 3. Quarterbacks (Football)—United States—Biography—Juvenile literature. I. Title.
  GV939.M2887T67 2012
  796.332092–dc23
  [B]

                          2011020413

Printed in the United States of America

062011 Lake Book Manufacturing, Inc., Melrose Park, IL

10 9 8 7 6 5 4 3 2 1

To Our Readers: We have done our best to make sure all Internet Addresses in this book were active and appropriate when we went to press. However, the author and the publisher have no control over and assume no liability for the material available on those Internet sites or on links to other Web sites. Any comments or suggestions can be sent by e-mail to comments@enslow.com or to the address on the back cover.

Every effort has been made to locate all copyright holders of material used in this book. If any errors or omissions have occurred, corrections will be made in future editions of this book.

Photo Credits: AP Images/AJ Mast, p. 15; AP Images/Bill Kostroun, p. 4; AP Images/David Drapkin, pp. 1, 10, 11, 12, 13, 14; AP Images/David Duprey, pp. 16–17, 20; AP Images/Ed Reinke, p. 9; AP Images/Kevin Terrell, p. 21; AP Images/NFL Photos, p. 7; AP Images/Paul Spinelli, pp. 18–19, 22; AP Images/Rogelio Solis, p. 8; AP Images/Thomas E. Witte, p. 6.

Cover Photo: AP Images/David Drapkin

Contents

Words to Know

pass—A throw from a quarterback in football.

quarterback—The player who throws the ball. Sometimes he hands the ball to another player who will run with it.

receiver—A player who runs down the field and tries to catch the ball.

Super Bowl—The championship game of football.

tackle—When one player throws his arms around another player and brings him to the ground.

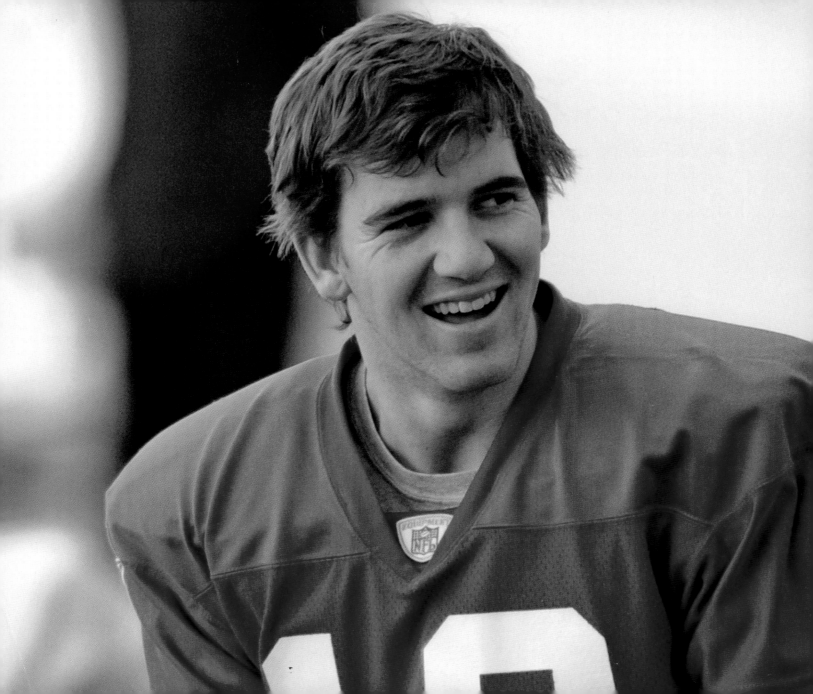

Eli Manning was born on January 3, 1981. He is the quarterback for the New York Giants.

The Manning family loves to play football. Eli's brother Peyton (left) is quarterback for the Indianapolis Colts. Their father, Archie Manning (right), was a quarterback, too.

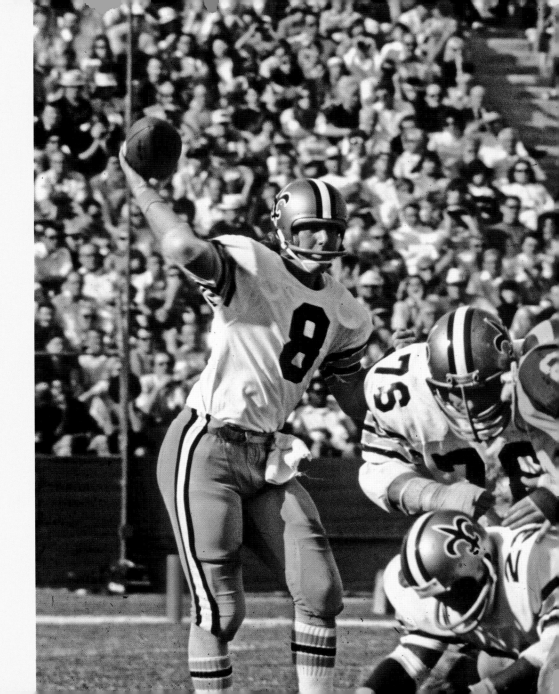

Eli played college football at Ole Miss. He had to learn how to take a hit. He also learned plays from his coaches.

9

Eli has a strong
arm. He can pass
the ball very far.
Sometimes he needs
to run with the ball.

Eli has to shout the play to his teammates. He looks across the whole field before choosing where to pass.

Sometimes Eli hands off to his teammate instead of passing. Other times, Eli must run to avoid being tackled!

14

In 2008, the Giants had to beat the Packers in Green Bay to make the Super Bowl. It was freezing cold. But the Giants won!

The Giants had to play the New England Patriots in the Super Bowl. The Patriots had not lost a game all year!

The Giants are running out of time. Eli throws a long pass. The receiver catches the ball and holds on! The Giants win the Super Bowl!

Eli held up the trophy after the game. A few days later, the team led a parade in New York City. Eli hopes to win another Super Bowl soon!

Further Reading

Diprimio, Pete. *Eli Manning*. Bear, Del.: Mitchell Lane, 2008.

Tieck, Sarah. *Eli Manning: Football Star*. Edina, Minn.:
   ABDO Publishing Company, 2011.

Internet Address

Eli Manning—Giants.com

http://www.giants.com/team/player34.html

INDEX

24